Dreaming Divine Dreams

H. Blundell
27· 03· 2018

DR. D. K. OLUKOYA

(2) Dr. D. K. OLUKOYA

DREAMING DIVINE DREAMS
© 2009 DR. D. K. OLUKOYA
ISBN 978-978-8424-03-1
November 2009

Published by:
The Battle Cry Christian Ministries
322, Herbert Macaulay Way, Yaba P. O. Box 12272, Ikeja,
Lagos.
website: www.battlecrychristianministries.org
email: info@battlecrychristianministries.org
Phone: 234(0)8033044239, 234(0)8033060073,

All Scripture quotation is from the King James Version of the
Bible

TABLE OF CONTENTS

CHAPTER ONE

DREAMING DIVINE DREAMS

And he said, Hear now my words: If there be a prophet among you, I the LORD will make myself known unto him in a vision, and will speak unto him in a dream. Numbers 12:6.

God can speak to you in a dream. It is possible for Him to communicate with you and give you directions in your dream. It will be a wonderful experience if He can speak to you in clear terms in your dreams. He is not talkative. He does not waste His words. He means what He says and says what He means. There is a man in the Bible called Jacob.

A DESTINY CHANGING DREAM

Part of his story is reproduced below:

And Jacob went out from Beer-sheba, and went toward Haran. And he lighted upon a certain place, and tarried there all night, because the sun was set; and he took of the stones of that place, and put them for his pillows, and lay down in that place to sleep. And he dreamed, and behold a ladder set up on the earth, and the top of it reached to heaven: and behold the angels of God ascending and descending on it. And, behold, the LORD stood above it, and said, I am the LORD God of Abraham thy father, and the God of Isaac: the land whereon thou liest, to thee will I give it, and to thy seed; And thy seed shall be as the dust of the earth, and thou shalt spread abroad to the west, and to the east, and to the north, and to the south: and in thee and in thy seed shall all the families of the earth be blessed. And, behold, I am with thee, and will keep thee in all places whither thou goest, and will bring thee again into this land; for I will not leave thee, until I have done that which I have spoken to thee of. And Jacob awaked out of his sleep, and he said, Surely the LORD is in this place; and I knew it not. Genesis 28:10-16.

Jacob was in a mess. He ran away from home for the fear of being killed. He ran away from a man called Laban. Later he showed that he was a fraudulent man and Laban dealt with him He changed Jacob's salary 10 times; he gave him the wrong wife.

Jacob was confused and at that level he had a dream. If your life is in a mess, God can come to you in your dream with a solution. God revealed the destiny of Jacob to him in his dream. The dream changed his life forever.

JOSEPH'S DREAM

The most popular dreamer was Joseph. Read about his dreams below:

And when his brethren saw that their father loved him more than all his brethren, they hated him, and could not speak peaceably unto him. And Joseph dreamed a dream, and he told it his brethren: and they hated him yet the more. And he said unto them, Hear, I pray you, this dream which I have dreamed: For, behold, we were binding sheaves in the field, and, lo, my sheaf arose, and also stood upright; and, behold, your sheaves stood round about, and made obeisance to my sheaf. And his brethren said to him, Shalt thou indeed reign over us? or shalt thou indeed have dominion over us? And they hated him yet the more for his dreams, and for his words. And he dreamed yet another dream, and told it his brethren, and said, Behold, I have dreamed a dream more; and, behold, the sun and the moon and the eleven stars made obeisance to me. And he told it to his father, and to his brethren: and his father rebuked him, and said unto him, What is this dream that thou hast dreamed? Shall I and thy mother and thy brethren indeed come to bow down ourselves to thee to the earth? And his brethren envied him; but his father observed the saying. Genesis 37:4-11.

Joseph dreamed a dream that showed him his future, the dream that guided his future. When his brethren threw him into a pit he knew that it was not the end of his destiny. Through these Bible passages, you can see that the Almighty communicates through dreams. The Bible says:

But while he thought on these things, behold, the angel of the Lord appeared unto him in a dream, saying, Joseph, thou son of David, fear not to take unto thee Mary thy wife: for that which is conceived in her is of the Holy Ghost. Matthew 1:20.

But when Herod was dead, behold, an angel of the Lord appeareth in a dream to Joseph in Egypt, Matthew 2:19.

Jesus Christ was taken to Egypt because of a dream. It is good to know that when Jesus left Israel he came to Africa. The Bible says:

But this is that which was spoken by the prophet Joel; And it shall come to pass in the last days, saith God, I will pour out of my Spirit upon all flesh: and your sons and your daughters shall prophesy, and your young men shall see visions, and your old men shall dream dreams. Acts 2:16-17.

The Bible makes us to understand that there are Holy Ghost-inspired dreams. If you are blessed with Holy Ghost-inspired dreams there is no way you will not overcome and overshadow your contemporaries. God communicates with you in your dreams and by the time you wake up your ideas will change positively.

DIVINE VISIONS

By the time a person is 60 years old, he would have slept for 20 years. One third of your life is spent sleeping. Dreams are visions during sleep. It is saddening that many people ignore what occupies one third of their lives.

A dream is a revelation given to man of a portion of the activities of the spirit realm. It is a spiritual monitor that tells you what is going on in your life in the spirit realm. I can tell you that 99 per cent of the revelation knowledge you need to overcome your problems can be received in the dreams.

God can reveal everything to you in the dream. To be informed is to be transformed. As you have knowledge, you will begin to recover. Dreams are means of revelation and they are the central way, God has chosen to be communicating with you. Through them He can reveal to you the plans of your destiny.

He can reveal to you the destiny of your family, your nation and your career.

In these last days, dreams are parts of prophetic outpouring of God's power upon His people. Your Joseph's dreams must come to pass. The dream of Joseph took him from the prison to the palace. Any man who is in a mess needs to dream the dream of Jacob. Any man who wants uncommon success must have his personal Joseph's dream.

YOUR FUTURE

Your Joseph's dream allows you to see your future. Your Joseph's dream is the heavenly picture of your destiny shown to you. Your Joseph's dream is the awareness of what you are supposed to be but you are not. You Joseph's dream is the divine goal planted into your spirit. Your Joseph's dream is your divine destination on earth.

Your Joseph's dream is the mountain top from which you can see your destiny afar off. Do you have a problem in your life? You need your Joseph's dream.

(12) Dr. D. K. OLUKOYA

Your Joseph's dream is the light that will shine in your way when you are in a valley of difficulty.

A sister prayed and had a dream where God brought and placed side by side her two-year old son and a 20- year old boy. God said to her: "This is your son. In the next 20 years this is the way he will be. He will engage himself in what he is not supposed to and will end up with a bad life. But if you don't want him to be like that there is a friend who often comes to look for him. Stop that so-called friend from coming to see him. The sister woke up and took heed to what the Lord said. Something happened 18 years later when the sister's son was around 20. The boy that the sister stopped coming to visit him was shot for armed robbery. If the boy had followed that friend it would have been a bad case.

DIVINE DIRECTION

Your Joseph's dream is the embodiment of your destiny. You need your Joseph's dream because there are treasures in the market place of your life which you need to discover. In the last days, God's people shall dream divine dreams and you must key into them. The Lord whom you serve shall suddenly come into His temple.

Many years ago, when I was still in school, we had a course called organic chemistry. It was very difficult. I had two big note books on this course. The first book was full. The second was about half full. We were to write an examination. Before that I had a dream where I saw an angel of God in a white garment brought two note books to me. He kept note book one at the back and gave me note book two. I forgot about the dream. One day, after a lecture I discovered that somebody had stolen notebook one. This meant that I would not read it for the examination.

I panicked because nobody was ready to give me a photocopy of the stolen notebook. I went home dejected. But I took my second note book, read it and also prayed. Then the Lord reminded me of my dream. On the day of the examination, question papers were distributed and to my surprise, none of the questions

(14) Dr. D. K. OLUKOYA

came from what I copied in note book one which was double the size of note book two that I read. At that level I felt sorry for the man who stole my note book one. For he must have wasted his time reading it.

A dream can chart your ways, guide your steps and give you information about your destiny. It is the will of God that you dream the dream of your destiny. But it is the agenda of the enemy for you not to have such dreams.

Some people have nightmares instead of divine dreams. Some even have dreams that will move them backwards instead of those that will take them forward.

Every dream has a message. There is no dream that does not have a message. You need to be a friend of God, so that He can communicate to you in your dreams. If you are a friend of iniquity and sin those are the things you will see in your dreams. Make friend with God today and you will dream divine dreams.

PRAYER POINTS

1. Enemies of my Joseph's dream, die, in the name of Jesus.

2. Dreams that will change my life, manifest, in the name of Jesus.

(16) Dr. D. K. OLUKOYA

CHAPTER TWO

YOUR DREAM AND YOUR DESTINY

And Jacob went out from Beer-sheba, and went toward Haran. And he lighted upon a certain place, and tarried there all night, because the sun was set; and he took of the stones of that place, and put them for his pillows, and lay down in that place to sleep. And he dreamed, and behold a ladder set up on the earth, and the top of it reached to heaven: and behold the angels of God ascending and descending on it. And, behold, the LORD stood above it, and said, I am the LORD God of Abraham thy father, and the God of Isaac: the land whereon thou liest, to thee will I give it, and to thy seed; And thy seed shall be as the dust of the earth, and thou shalt spread abroad to the west, and to the east, and to the north, and to the south: and in thee and in thy seed shall all the families of the earth be blessed. And, behold, I am with thee, and will keep thee in all places whither thou goest, and will bring thee again into this land; for I will not leave thee, until I have done that which I have spoken to thee of. And Jacob awaked out of his sleep, and he said,

Surely the LORD is in this place; and I knew it not. Genesis 28:10-16.

You need a Jacob's dream when you are confused. You need a Jacob's dream when the enemy rises against you. You need a Jacob's dream when you don't know where to go. You need a Jacob's dream when household wickedness is against you. You need a Jacob's dream when people are cheating you and are taking what belongs to you. You need a Jacob's dream when you know you are a king, but you have no crown and no palace.

THE NEED OF THE HOUR

You need a Jacob's dream when you notice that where you are is not where you are supposed to be. You need a Jacob's dream when you lack information about your destiny from heaven. You need a Jacob's dream when you know that going forward is a problem and going backward also is a problem. Every man who wants to win in life needs a Jacob's dream.

How wonderful will it be if God can communicate with you in your dream and tell you to do this or that. You will never be poor in your life. This is the reason Jacob's dream is needed. After Jacob had the dream, his life was not the same again. There are dreams you can have and they will change your life forever.

Every man who wants uncommon success must have his personal Joseph's dream. Joseph's dream is the heavenly picture of your life. Your Joseph's dream is the awareness of what you are to be but you are not. Your Joseph's dream is the video film of your correct life revealed in heaven.

YOUR TREASURE

Your Joseph's dream is that pathway that you will use to circumvent the valley of the shadow of difficulty. Your Joseph's dream is the treasure of your marketplace in your life. It is tragic when a treasure is looking for treasure. You are a treasure, so you should stop looking for a treasure.

One day, a poor, God-fearing Jew living in a

(20) Dr. D. K. OLUKOYA

particular city had a dream that he was at the base of a bridge leading to the king's palace. The dream revealed to him that there was a treasure buried in that spot that could make him rich for the rest of his life. He stood up and travelled to the place. But when he got there, he found that it was heavily guarded by soldiers. He did not know what to do. He kept roaming around there for two weeks.

One day, one of the soldiers recognised him as somebody who had been constantly roaming around that area and arrested him for being a spy. The Jew told the soldier why he kept roaming around the place. He was surprised that the soldier laughed at him instead of beating him and putting him in prison.

The soldier told him that he also had a dream that the Jew found a treasure on his roof and told him to go home. When he got home and checked his roof, he saw the treasure that wiped away poverty from his life. That Jew had to go to that location to get information on how to find his treasure and he found it. May you find yours!

A man had a dream that an angel of God was with him showing him good things in heaven, but suddenly he saw a man looking fresh, full of anointing and very vibrant. He asked the angel who the man was and the angel said it was he. The man was the correct version of him in heaven. But he was not living up to the standard. If he was to be compared with the vibrant man, he would be 23 years younger. He woke up realising that instead of killing lions and tigers he was busy killing mosquitoes.

DREAM PATTERNS

There are basically six kinds of dreams:

1. *Dreams that add to you:* When you have this kind of a dream, your lots get improved.

2. *Dreams that subtract from you:* When you have these kind of dreams, they diminish you.

3. *Dreams that leave you the way they met you:* These kinds of dreams will not move you forward and will not take you backward. You will just remain the same.

4. Dreams that empty you.

A 25-year-old man based in the US dreamt that he got married to their school caterer. There was nothing bad in the dream but he was 25 and the caterer was 66. As the devil arranged it, the boy went to the cafeteria and the woman laughed at him and gave him free food. That was how he concluded that the dream was true and they got married.

The boy was a Nigerian, but the white woman a German. Later, he discovered that the woman was a strange woman. At night she would be lifted up from the bed and he would be on the bed watching her being lifted up and whenever she came down she would be as strong as a 20-year-old girl. The boy was afraid to tell his parents and he began to grow thin.

However, somebody sent him a copy of our book, Prayer Rain, and he prayed some of the prayers there and read the book of Psalms. At night, as the woman was lifted up by strange powers as usual, he started praying and the woman fell on the bed and got angry with him. From that night the boy's problem started.

5. *Dreams that catapult you destiny:* Many people have had dreams and their lives are no longer the same.

6. *Dreams that waste you.*

The best dreams are the dreams that add to you and the dreams that catapult you. Such dreams will automatically make you become a champion. All dreams have messages and we have to know the messages. They are guidelines to your destiny.

THE EVIL COBWEB

I came from a very poor home. When I was a bachelor, I lived in a kind of house usually filled with tenants with different spirits. One day, I had a dream that one of the tenants was weaving cobweb in front of my room. The dream gave me a signal, so when I got a scholarship to study abroad, I never bothered telling anybody. When I got my visa, ticket and every other document, I told nobody. I kept this to myself for good six months because the dream had given me a signal.

(24) Dr. D. K. OLUKOYA

On the exact day of my departure, I moved my belongings, took my box and put on the suit I bought. Some tenants saw me and asked where I was going. I told them I was travelling. They asked if I just knew about it. I told them I knew long ago but I did not want to tell anybody. If I had told them they would have arranged a cobweb that would prevent me from travelling. You will always get information through your divine dreams.

When I was abroad studying, one of my lecturers and my supervisor, a white man, kept on saying I should take a break for one month to visit my parents in Nigeria. When I got home one night, I had a dream that I was at the Muritala Mohammed Airport and my flight was announced to travel back to the United Kingdom. But when I stood up to go where the flight was, it had already left. The next day, I told my lecturer that I was not going home. He asked if I didn't like my parents. I told him I did but that I was not going home.

He urged me to go for two weeks but I insisted on staying back. All the Nigerians who went home for that holiday could not come back to the UK because there was a military coup in Nigeria which led to the closure of the airport. This incident disrupted the programme of some of them. Some missed their examination and some had to repeat their courses. What delivered me was the dream that I had.

WHY GOD USES DREAMS

Why does God use dreams to communicate when He can use other means? The reasons are:

1. People's minds get easily clouded with businesses or other issues during the day.

2. The only quiet time some people have is when sleeping.

3. When you are asleep, your conscious mind cannot block God's message.

4. When you are awake, your conscious mind will not allow you to get God's message. It blocks the way of hearing from God.

5. When we are asleep, God is able to do things

(26) Dr. D. K. OLUKOYA

we cannot contest.

6. When you are asleep, you lose control of your life and God takes over.

7. God can appear in your dream to warn you. The Bible says:

For God speaketh once, yea twice, yet man perceiveth it not. In a dream, in a vision of the night, when deep sleep falleth upon men, in slumberings upon the bed; Then he openeth the ears of men, and sealeth their instruction, That he may withdraw man from his purpose, and hide pride from man. He keepeth back his soul from the pit, and his life from perishing by the sword. Job 33:14-18.

It was in the dream that Pharaoh got the revelation that there would be famine in Egypt. He had to call Joseph to explain the dream. God warns you in the dream in order for you not to go wrong.

God uses dreams to prevent you from evil. He told Joseph in the dream to take the Baby Jesus to Egypt to avert trouble for the Baby. When Herod was dead,

God told Joseph in the dream to take the Baby back to his rightful location. It is in the dream that God prevents you from going to hell fire.

How can you have an encounter with God in your dreams?

1. *Make God your friend:* This means that you must live a pure life and be free from sins that can keep God far away from you. If you live a dirty life, you will always have a dirty dream. If your life is unclean, your dream will be unclean. The Bible says, "If you move close to me, I will move closer to you. And if you move far away from me, I will move farther away from you." You have to make God your friend.

2. *You must ask God for divine dreams:* Whosoever asks shall receive.

3. *Deal with your thought life:* As a man thinketh in his heart so is he.

4. *Emulate the saints of the old who had divine encounter with God:* Forget things of

the past and move forward. Be like Abraham who put his faith in God. Be like Enoch who daily walked in fellowship with God. Be like Moses who chose to suffer rather than enjoy the pleasures of the world. Be like Daniel who communed with God at all times. Be like Isaiah and consecrate yourself to God.

Be like John and lean on the bosom of the Master. Be like Stephen and manifest a forgiving spirit to those who hurt you. Be like the heavenly hosts and form the habit of praising God at all times. When you emulate all these, God will visit you in your dreams and you will become a divine dreamer.

PRAYER POINTS

1. In my dreams, Oh God, appear, in the name of Jesus.

2. Where is the Lord God of Elijah, arise, appear in my dream, in the name of Jesus.

3. Dreams of detention and demotion, die, in the name of Jesus.

4. My Jacob's dream, arise and locate me, in the name of Jesus.

5. Witchcraft appearance in my dream, you are a liar. Die, in the name of Jesus.

(30) Dr. D. K. OLUKOYA

CHAPTER THREE

THE DREAM CONDITIONERS

But while he thought on these things, behold, the angel of the Lord appeared unto him in a dream, saying, Joseph, thou son of David, fear not to take unto thee Mary thy wife: for that which is conceived in her is of the Holy Ghost. Matthew 1:20.

Dreams are locations where angels of the Lord appear. Demons and terrible things cannot appear when the angels of the Lord are appearing. The bottom line is that God can give you an instruction in your dream. The Bible says;

And it shall come to pass in the last days, saith God, I will pour out of my Spirit upon all flesh: and your sons and your daughters shall prophesy, and your young men shall see visions, and your old men shall dream dreams: Acts 2:17.

The Bible passage above makes it clear that in the last days the ministry of dreams and visions shall increase and be used to guide the children of God accordingly.

(32) Dr. D. K. OLUKOYA

DREAM SIGNALS

Dreams are deep symbols about life. Sometimes they are dark sayings. A dream can be a prophetic word. It can be a word of knowledge and wisdom. It can reveal edification and warning. It can reveal your future and can give you an insight of what is going to happen in your later years.

Your intimacy with Jesus will greatly determine your ability to hear from Him through your dreams. The greater your intimacy with Jesus Christ, the greater your level of ability to receive information in the dream. A dream can endow you with the spirit of intercession and can give you a burden to pray for a particular person or event.

Dreams enable you to look into the realm of the spirit. They can sometimes be true, neutral or false. But God reveals himself to men through dreams. It is easy to tell the originality and the authenticity of a dream. Whether a dream is of good origin or authentic can only be determined when we recognise who receives glory after the dream. If at the end of the dream, Jesus Christ is not glorified then the dream is an evil dream.

Dreams can give assurance, encouragement, direction, instruction and guidance. They can convey a revelation, a plan and strategy of God's purpose for your life. This is the reason some dreams require interpretations. Some interpretations are given during the dreams or when you wake up.

THE REALM OF DREAMS

Beloved, the land of the dream is as important as the land of the physical. One way or the other you are a product of your dream. Dreams are not to be ignored or pushed aside. Basically, dreams are spiritual monitors telling you what is going on in your life in the spirit realm. They never lie because they contain a message. Your dreams never lie.

Satan, the devil, knows the importance of dreams to mankind. He tries to influence dreams that are why he attacks people with sickness and all kinds of tragedies in the dream. He can transform into an

(34) Dr. D. K. OLUKOYA

angel of light to deceive the believer in the dream. Every dream has a meaning. Even if it appeared disorganised and as nonsense, it still has a meaning. In your dream, your spirit breaks into the spirit realm.

Dream interpretation is purely a gift from God. Dreams cannot be figured out with human understanding. You can ask for the gift from God. You can however learn some principles by which you can interpret what you see.

THE GIFT OF DREAMS

The language of dreams is one of God's most neglected gifts to man. Mankind tends to push it aside as if it were nothing. An average person sleeps about eight hours daily which means that one third of our lives is spent sleeping. This means that if you are 30 years old, you have spent 10 years of your life sleeping.

If you are a good student of the Bible, you will find out that there are over 250 references to dreams.

There are different types of dreams.

1. *Reminder dreams:* These bring things that will make you remember.

2. *Repetitive dreams:* These keep on telling you that there is something you have not addressed. They keep repeating themselves.

3. *Predictive dreams.* These can tell you what is about to happen.

The point is that in these last days dreams will be intensified, especially spiritually deep dreams. They will intensify to a level where some believers will be ushered into greatness. The Bible says that old men shall dream dreams. In the Scriptures, dreams are frequent and continual.

There are dreams you remember with clarity when you wake up and there are dreams you just remember faintly. Very many people receive deliverance through the messages they listened to in their dreams.

When you have the right dreams it can bring healing to your personal, professional, career or spiritual life. Where most people have trouble is when

(36) Dr. D. K. OLUKOYA

the dreams appear to be parables. Some dreams are like parables of Jesus which have deeper meaning.

Many dreams are the sub-conscious shouting at you. A dream sometimes comes to you to address an issue you are ignoring. It brings to attention your areas of tension or unresolved areas. It can be a place of encounter. Dreams are New Testaments. They are also used as God's means of having an encounter with man. They can empower, protect and guide you. They have transforming powers and God speaks to man through them.

KILLER DREAMS

There is what can be termed killer dreams. They are:

1. *Seeing corpses, coffins or attending a funeral.* You must kill it immediately you wake up.

2. *Being handcuffed or chained.*

3. *Marriage to an unknown person.*

4. *Begging for food and there is no money.*

5. *Walking about barefooted.*

6. *Wearing torn or ragged clothes.*

7. *Somebody trying to cut your hair.*

8. *Seeing vultures around you.*

9. *Driving a vehicle which stops and refuses to start.*

10. *Being pursued by wild animals.*

11. *Discussing and eating with dead relatives.*

You must kill all these killer dreams. When they pursue you, you pursue them.

12. *Holding a Bible and somebody grabbing it and you cannot find both the person and the Bible.*

13. *Eating your own vomit.*

14. *Seeing yourself or your relatives on the hospital bed.*

15. *When you find yourself crying or weeping.*

16. *Losing a large sum of money.*

(38) Dr. D. K. OLUKOYA

17. *Gunshot and bullets pursuing you.*

18. *Bitten by animals.*

19. *Roaming about the marketplace.*

20. *Carrying a big load that does not belong to you.*

21. *Masquerade pursuing you around.* Every masquerade dream that a black man has represents ancestral powers. You need to kill them.

22. *Swimming.*

23. *Having sex with an unknown person.*

24. *When somebody is showing you a bottle of blood.*

25. *When you eat what you don't eat in the physical realm.*

DREAM INDICATORS

What factors influence your dream life?

1. *Your level of purity:*

Your level of holiness and brokenness will determine your kind of dream. Holy people have holy dreams. Your level of purity in the body, the soul and the spirit determine your dream life.

2. *How much of the flesh controls your life*

If you yield to the flesh all the time, you will have a serious war in the dream.

3. *Bad company*

If your friends are children of the devil, you will have bad dreams because they will influence your life.

4. *Your foundation and background*

If your father is not a good Christian and your mother is not the type that has time for the Lord, then you will have bad dreams.

5. *Whether you are under curses and evil covenants*

When you are under a terrible curse or covenants,

(40) Dr. D. K. OLUKOYA

you will always have terrible dreams.

6. *The kinds of enemies you are fighting*

The more terrible the kind of enemies you are fighting, the worse your dream life becomes.

7. *The level of the word of God in you*

The level of the word of God in you decides the kinds of dreams you will have.

8. *What you eat and drink can condition your dream life.*

9. *Environmental factor*

When you live in a cursed house or your business is located in a demon possessed place, this will affect and determine your dream life.

10. *Cultural orientation*

This is why some people dream of returning to their places of birth. It can condition or affect your dream life.

11. *Past sexual associates*

This also conditions your dream life.

12. *Past involvement in the occult*

If you were a cultist, or a lodge member; this can influence your dream life.

13. *Level of the spiritual lives of your parents*

If your parents are very prayerful, their prayers can help your dream life.

14. *Sickness and illness.*

15. *Level of satanic oppression which you have gone through*

The higher the oppression, the more horrible the dreams.

16. *Incisions on the body*

Incisions on your body give the enemy access to your blood. They can condition your dream life.

17. *Worry and anxiety*

18. *Incomplete deliverance*

If your deliverance is not completed, you may have small respite and your problem comes back. This can influence your dream life.

19. *Sleep disturbance.*

20. *Strategic position in God's agenda.*

21. *Your level of brokenness.*

If you don't know these major dream conditioners, visions may become nightmares. Dreams that will move you forward may become dreams that will demote you. Dreams of warning can become dreams of tragedy. Dreams of glory can become dreams of shame. You must deal with any spirit preventing you from entering into the realm of your dream life.

PRAYER POINTS

1. Dream kidnappers, dream criminals, die, in the name of Jesus.

2. I fire back every arrow of the enemy from my dream, in the name of Jesus.

3. Killer dreams, I am not your candidate. Die, in the name of Jesus.

Other Publications by Dr. D. K. Olukoya

1. 100 Facts About Idolatry
2. A-Z of Complete Deliverance
3. Be Prepared
4. Bewitchment must die
5. Biblical Principles of Dream Interpretation
6. Born Great, But Tied Down
7. Breaking Bad Habits
8. Breakthrough Prayers For Business Professionals
9. Bringing Down The Power of God
10. Brokenness
11. Can God?
12. Can God Trust You?
13. Command The Morning
14. Consecration Commitment & Loyalty
15. Contending For The Kingdom
16. Connecting To The God of Breakthroughs
17. Criminals In The House Of God
18. Dancers At The Gate of Hell
19. Dealing With Hidden Curses
20. Dealing With Local Satanic Technology
21. Dealing With Satanic Exchange
22. Dealing With The Evil Powers Of Your Father's House
23. Dealing With Tropical Demons
24. Dealing With Unprofitable Roots
25. Dealing With Witchcraft Barbers
26. Deliverance By Fire

40

Other Publications by Dr. D. K. Olukoya

42

43

44

Other Publications by Dr. D. K. Olukoya

Other Publications by Dr. D. K. Olukoya

YORUBA PUBLICATIONS
1. ADURA AGBAYORI
2. ADURA TI NSI OKE NIDI
3. OJO ADURA

FRENCH PUBLICATIONS
1. PLUIE DE PRIERE
2. ESPIRIT DE VAGABONDAGE
3. EN FINIR AVEC LES FORCES MALEFIQUES DE LA MAISON DE TON PERE
4. QUE I'ENVOUTEMENT PERISSE
5. FRAPPEZ I'ADVERSAIRE ET IL FUIRA
6. COMMENT RECEVIOR LA DELIVRANCE DU MARI ET FEMME DE NUIT
7. CPMMENT SE DELIVRER SOI-MEME
8. POVOIR CONTRE LES TERRORITES SPIRITUEL
9. PRIERE DE PERCEES POUR LES HOMMES D'AFFAIRES
10. PRIER JUSQU'A REMPORTER LA VICTOIRE
11. PRIERES VIOLENTES POUR HUMILIER LES PROBLEMES OPINIATRES
12. PRIERE POUR DETRUIRE LES MALADIES ET INFIRMITES
13. LE COMBAT SPIRITUEL ET LE FOYER
14. BILAN SPIRITUEL PERSONNEL
15. VICTOIRES SUR LES REVES SATANIQUES

Other Publications by Dr. D. K. Olukoya

ANNUAL 70 DAYS PRAYER AND FASTING PUBLICATIONS

Other Publications by Dr. D. K. Olukoya

2. Let God Answer By Fire
3. Prayers To Mount With Wings As Eagles
4. Prayers That Bring Explosive Increase
5. Prayers For Open Heavens
6. Prayers To Make You Fulfil Your Divine Destiny
7. Prayers That Make God To Answer And Fight By Fire
8. Prayers That Bring Unchallengeable Victory And Breakthrough Rainfall Bombardments
9. Prayers That Bring Dominion Prosperity And Uncommon Success
10. Prayers That Bring Power And Overflowing Progress
11. Prayers That Bring Laughter And Enlargement Breakthroughs
12. Prayers That Bring Uncommon Favour And Breakthroughs
13. Prayers That Bring Unprecedented Greatness & Unmatchable Increase
14. Prayers That Bring Awesome Testimonies And Turn Around Breakthroughs

28675781R00031

Printed in Great Britain
by Amazon